KAREN F. WILLIAMS

presents

Lights, Drama, Worship

Plays, Sketches, & Readings for the Church

KAREN F. WILLIAMS

presents

Lights, Drama, Worship!

Plays, Sketches, & Readings for the Church

ZONDERVAN™

GRAND RAPIDS, MICHIGAN 49530 USA

ZONDERVAN™

Lights, Drama, Worship! Volume 3
Copyright © 2004 by Karen F. Williams

Requests for information should be addressed to:
Zondervan, *Grand Rapids, Michigan 49530*

Library of Congress Cataloging-in-Publication Data

Williams, Karen F., 1959–
Lights, drama, worship! / Karen F. Williams.—1st ed.
    p. cm.
Includes bibliographical references and index.
    ISBN 0-310-24245-2 (volume 1)—ISBN 0-310-24249-5 (volume 2)—
    ISBN 0-310-24263-0 (volume 3)—ISBN 0-310-24264-9 (volume 4)
    1. Drama in Christian education. 2. Christian drama, American. I. Title.
BV1534.4.W55 2004
246'.72—dc22

2003014726

Interior design by Susan Ambs

Printed in the United States of America

03 04 05 06 07 08 09 /❖ ML/ 10 9 8 7 6 5 4 3 2 1

To the Williamses, the Murchisons, and the Robinsons,
who have given me a lifetime of family support

Contents

Who's Who in the Cast

The theatre is an art which reposes upon the work of many collaborators. . . . We have been accustomed to think that a work of art is by definition the product of one governing selecting will.

Thornton Wilder

A play requires a cast of people to produce. So it was with the writing of this volume. Numerous persons played leading roles in bringing these plays to the published stage.

The Director— All glory and thanks to God, my Divine Director, for originating this work's vision and providing the wherewithal to complete it.

Manuscript Evaluators— Edna Brown, James Lawrence, and Denise Owens, I am deeply indebted to you for spending extensive time evaluating this volume and offering invaluable guidance, constructive criticism, editorial support, and many kind words of encouragement.

Reviewers— I offer gratitude for my dear colleagues who spent time reviewing one or more plays and providing significant feedback: Gwendolyn Colvin, Darrell and Tracey Edwards, Joan Daniel, Regina Hoosier, Lilly Lester, and Tonya Williams.

Family and Friends— Deep appreciation goes to devoted family members whose constant prayers and inspiring words provided strength for my journey. Thanks to Arnetta Robinson, Ann Williams, and Fred and

JoAnneWilliams, who read portions of this volume. I'm also grateful for the prayers of numerous friends who graciously asked, "How's the writing going?" Angela Denmark and Delores Steele, thanks for being faithful friends who not only read sections of the manuscript but also offered your prayers, insightful words, and were always willing to assist with this writing project every step along the way.

Pastors and Drama Ministry— Pastors Horace and Kiwanis Hockett, thanks for being dramatists whose lives exemplify holiness, excellence, and humility. Pastor Hockett, I'm most appreciative of your reading several plays and offering kind words of support. Also thanks to Director Lawrence James and Living Parables members for your generous support and for providing an avenue for me to present my writings. Special thanks to "Black Women Walking" staged readers Marcie Hockett, Dorothy Dobson, and Carol Wade, and "Tongue Twisters" performers Leslie Poston and Anthony Jones.

The Producers— Many thanks to the outstanding staff at Zondervan. I'm most appreciative of Jim Ruark, my editor, who graciously guided me through each publishing phase and was always available to respond to my questions and concerns. Special thanks to Alicia Mey and the splendid marketing staff for your expertise and creativity.

The Cast and Production Staff— I offer my appreciation to all who purchase this volume and transform this print from page to stage. Thank you kindly, for you are the ones who bring these written expressions to life.

Introduction

What are you looking at me for?
I didn't come to stay.
I just came to say Happy Easter Day!

I remember young children saying this rhyme for Easter programs when I was a child. This amusing speech, normally recited by a child five years old or younger, always received warm smiles and laughter from the congregation, followed by thunderous applause. I too had my share of giving recitations, which was my least favorite thing to do. The Sunday school department gave all the children short speeches, normally a week before the program. So I practiced my speech—consisting of four to eight lines—all week long in front my family. I even asked my siblings to call my name. They would say, "We will now have a speech by Karen Williams." I would smile at the sound of my name, rise with confidence, stand in the middle of the living room floor, and recite with ease.

Soon the big program day arrived, and I had to leave the comfort of my living room. And with that departure, all my confidence left as well. At church I sat in my seat, my heart pounding with fear, waiting to hear my name. Finally I heard an adult voice at the front of the sanctuary announce those dreaded words: "Next we have a speech by Karen Williams." All eyes turned toward me, and at that moment I wanted to disappear. I arose and made the long walk to the front of the altar. Trembling with fear, I recited my speech quickly. As I made my way back to the pew, I heard a welcome sound, the congregation's applause. Before I knew it, I was in the comfort of my seat again, relieved that I had survived the public ordeal. Whew! That was a lot of work for just a few lines. This was my first experience with church drama—or perhaps more aptly, church *trauma*.

While recitations like the "Happy Easter Day" rhyme may not technically qualify as drama, they certainly capture our attention, which is one thing drama does. As I moved from recitations to acting in plays during my teenage years, I noticed how the congregation maintained rapt attention during a play. In my early twenties when I started writing plays for my church drama group, I began to see these performances as a form of ministry. Around that same time my relationship with Christ deepened, and I discovered that plays, even simple sketches, could touch lives in ways that sermons did not. I saw how the audience was able to identify with the characters onstage or relate to the subject. At times people would tell me that a particular play inspired them or made them examine their relationship with God.

A powerful play can both entertain and bring us into God's presence, moving us to worship. Two authors provide definitions of worship that best explain my heart and my purpose in writing these plays. First, James Burton Coffman:

> A good description of worship is that of Isaiah 6:1−8, an analysis of which shows that worship is: (1) an awareness of the presence of God, (2) a consciousness of sin and unworthiness on the part of the worshipper, (3) a sense of cleansing and forgiveness, and (4) a response of the soul with reference to doing God's will: "Here am I, send me!"[1]

The other definition comes from Rick Warren:

> Worship is not a *part* of your life; it *is* your life. Worship is not just
> for church services.... Every activity can be transformed into an act
> of worship when you do it for the praise, glory, and pleasure of God."[2]

Whether you encounter a cleansing and forgiveness, sense God's presence, or say, "Lord, here am I," my hope is that this volume of *Lights, Drama, Worship!* will provide your congregation with a powerful worship experience ... an experience that transcends the church setting and becomes a lifestyle.

In this volume you will find short, easy-to-perform readings for groups with little or no drama experience as well as longer, more structured plays for experienced drama ministries. These plays include four styles:

1. Dramatic reading/recitation ("A Mother's Love")
2. Readers theater ("What People Think")
3. Sketches ("The Christmas Story" and "The Curator")
4. Feature play ("The Husband Center")

I describe each style in Types of Drama in This Volume (pages 14–16). In Production Notes (pages 17–20), I suggest how to stage the plays and also include some production tips. If you desire to learn more about producing church plays, see the list of resources on page 20.

I have found certain steps to be effective in preparing to perform plays. As your drama team rehearses, you may want to follow these recommendations. First, I encourage you to spend time praying together. During your rehearsals, pray for unity and a team spirit within the group. Pray that God will be glorified through your cast and production team. Pray too that the play will inspire the congregation and allow them to experience God's presence. You may also want to set aside time to fast before the performance.

Next, take some time during your first or second rehearsal to talk about the play: What does the play say to you? Why is your character important in this play? What can you learn from your character? Why is the play's theme important? What effect might the play have on the congregation? Does the play reveal any insights about your relationship with God and others? This discussion will help your group understand the play's purpose and theme, allowing them to see the presentation as ministry.

Last, strive for excellence in your presentation. This means placing a premium on doing your best with the resources available to you and striving to present a quality production. Certainly, selecting a cast, arranging rehearsals suitable for everyone's schedule, and directing a play is no easy task. Yet by allowing adequate time for rehearsals, the production becomes manageable. My hope, then, is that when all is said and done—after spending time in prayer and after the long hours of production preparation—your drama team, in addition to your audience, will not only experience the presence of God but also develop a closer relationship with him.

Types of Drama in This Volume

Dramatic Reading and Readers Theater

A *dramatic reading,* also called an *interpretive reading,* presents one or more persons reading a script with purposeful vocal expression. Normally there are no or limited props and scenery, little or suggestive movement, and no memorization. The readers may use a black folder to hold their scripts or they may place the script on music stands or lecterns. Since the focus is on the words and ideas and not physical action, the readers must articulate their words clearly, precisely, and expressively. Some readings may involve a group, called a chorus, speaking simultaneously. Speaking in unison is important in these cases. In her book *Praising God through the Lively Arts,* Linda Goens offers helpful advice for group or choral reading:

In the beginning it is advisable to keep choral readers to a small number. The more people reading in chorus, the harder it is to read in unison and the more difficult for the congregation to understand the words and appreciate the type of reading. Start with three or four readers in chorus, increasing the number later.

There are three major concerns with choral reading that take special practice: beginning together with confidence, pacing, and inflection. The group needs to begin speaking in perfect unison, to pause together at punctuation and other designated points, and to speak with the same inflection (for example, loudly, softly, harshly, tenderly), emphasizing the same words in the same way, and so on.[3]

The dramatic reading in this volume, "A Mother's Love," is intended for children to perform.

Readers theater is similar to dramatic reading in that it does not typically require props, scenery, and movement. It too may include group or choral reading. However, readers theater presentations are usually longer and may include characters who move about the stage. Readers can perform by either standing or sitting on stools. They may also perform with or without memorization. When they memorize the script, they have the freedom to include some movement or hand gestures. Using music stands or lecterns to hold scripts is another way to free the readers' hands. If the script is not memorized, readers should be so familiar with their lines that they need only glance at the pages. Leslie Irene Coger and Melvin R. White, in their *Readers Theatre Handbook,* say that the eyes are the most expressive facial feature, helping to depict a character's attitude and communicate the reading's meaning while helping to maintain audience attention:

If the eyes are kept continuously on the page, the readers tend to turn the whole face downward, and as a result their voices are directed toward the floor and are difficult to hear. The readers should therefore keep their eyes as free of the script as possible. This does not mean that they ignore the script; rather, they must grasp the words in a quick glance so that they may use their eyes for expressive purposes.[4]

The dramatic reading "A Mother's Love" is a Mother's Day tribute that children age twelve or younger can perform. Black folders will not be needed for this reading since all lines should be memorized. "What People Think" is the readers theater presentation for this volume.

Sketches

Sketches have the structure of a play (characters, conflict, resolution) but are much shorter. Since acting is involved, sketches require characters to memorize their lines. Although scenery, props, and costumes may be used, they are normally kept to a minimum; the emphasis is on the message the sketch is conveying to the audience. Sketches can be serious, but more often than not they are humorous and range in performance time from two to twelve minutes. The two sketches in this volume are "The Christmas Story" and "The Curator."

Feature Play

The *feature play* is the longest dramatic form included here and therefore requires more production time to allow for extensive rehearsals and interpretation of lines, blocking (movement of characters), and stage preparation. This play is intended to be the main presentation for a worship service or program. "The Husband Center" is the feature play in this volume.

Production Notes and Tips

What Each Play Contains

Each play contains the following to assist you in production.

Scripture References: Bible passages in the play or Scriptures to support the theme

Theme: The play's topic or subject matter

Summary: A brief description of the play

Characters: The people involved in the play, or a list of actors (sometimes with character descriptions)

Costume Suggestions: Costume descriptions. Not all the plays include descriptions. These are merely suggestions; add costumes if it will present a better production.

Set Design: Scenery that gives the location and environment of the play; also an illustration of the stage layout. Since sanctuaries are not uniform in structure, the entrances and exits as I have indicated in the script may not work for your stage. Adjust the layout so that it works best for your church. The diagram on page 22 shows stage positions.

Props: A list of items used to enhance the set and the characters' actions

Setting: A description of the scene as the play begins (what props and furniture are onstage and where the characters are positioned). Sometimes the setting is a specific place such as a bookstore or a home. When it is not a designated place, I use the words "No particular place defined."

Rehearsal Notes: A place for the director, actors, and backstage persons to write rehearsal dates and other important information relative to the play

Music/Sound Effects: A list of songs, instrumentals, or sounds in the play (not all plays will include music)

Devotional Moment: A further explanation of the sketch, appropriate to be read by the pastor or program director after the performance. Two presentations ("What People Think" and "The Curator") in this volume conclude with a brief devotional. (Note: "The Curator" concludes with questions that are better suited for settings where discussion can take place.)

Helpful Tips from Other Dramatists

Warm-up Exercises

Exercises to help the actors relax and prepare their vocals for the stage are called warm-up exercises. The following suggestions are from *The Dramatic Arts in Ministry* by Ev Robertson.

1. Stretch muscles by reaching for the ceiling. Reach high several times with each hand stretching as much as possible. Then collapse from the waist and drop hands toward the floor. Hang as relaxed as possible. Repeat the exercise several times.
2. Shake hands rapidly from the wrist.
3. Shake arms from the shoulders.
4. Shake each leg.
5. Move head in a circle one direction and then the other.
6. Stretch facial muscles into grotesque shapes and then relax after each.
7. Combine basic vowel sounds (ah, eh, eee, ai, oh, oo) with explosive consonants and repeat rapidly. Example: bah, bah, bah; beh, beh, beh; bee, bee, bee; bai, bai, bai; boh, boh, boh; boo, boo, boo. Other consonants to use are tah, pah, lah, mah, nah, cah, etc.
8. Repeat nursery rhymes or tongue twisters. Example: "Peter Piper picked a peck of pickled peppers."[5]

Blocking Tips

Blocking is simply the movement of characters onstage. Charles M. Tanner in *Acting on Faith* (volume 1) provides these tips:

> You need movement to keep the play dynamic.
>
> You want to keep it balanced. (Don't have four characters all walk to the same side of the stage at the same time. Your stage will "sink.")
>
> Keep your performers open to the audience—eyes and faces visible—not only when they are speaking, but also when they are reacting to others.
>
> Motivate the movement. People do things for reasons. The characters in the play must move for reasons. The motivations can be mechanical (to get a cup of coffee), emotional (to hide their fear), psychological (they are lying), or intellectual (they are distracting someone).[6]

Rehearsals

Steve Pederson in *Drama Ministry* and Laura Martinez in *Drama for the Dramatically Challenged* offer advice for the director.

Pederson: "Directors need to view rehearsals as top priority. This means that we're prepared, we accomplish our goal, we use time efficiently, and we approach the work with an attitude of enjoyment. We are sensitive to the needs of different actors, we challenge, speak the truth in love, and encourage. It is a tall order. But it's important because the key to a good performance is good rehearsal."[7]

Martinez: "Point out that when an audience laughs, the players need to stay in character (as if the audience were not there) and at the same time try to sense the crescendo of the laughter. Beginning the next line of dialogue just as the laughter begins will cause many, if not most, of the audience to miss it. . . . While waiting for the laughter to die down actors should . . . attempt to keep the scene alive by using gestures and actions appropriate to their characters."[8]

RESOURCES FOR YOUR DRAMA MINISTRY

Linda M. Goens. *Praising God through the Lively Arts.* Nashville: Abingdon, 1999.

John Lewis, Laura Andrews, and Flip Kobler. *The Complete Guide to Church Play Production.* Nashville: Convention Press, 1997.

Laura I. Martinez. *Drama for the Dramatically Challenged: Church Plays Made Easy.* Valley Forge, PA: Judson Press, 2000.

Rory Noland. *The Heart of the Artist.* Grand Rapids: Zondervan, 1999.

Steve Pederson. *Drama Ministry: Practical Help for Making Drama a Vital Part of Your Church.* Grand Rapids: Zondervan, 1999.

NOTES

1. James Burton Coffman, *Commentary on John 4,* Coffman Commentaries on the Old and New Testament (Abilene, TX: Abilene Christian University Press, 1984).

2. Rick Warren, *The Purpose Driven Life* (Grand Rapids: Zondervan, 2002), 66–67.

3. Linda Goens, *Praising God through the Lively Arts* (Nashville: Abingdon, 1999), 35.

4. Leslie Irene Coger and Melvin R. White, *Readers Theatre Handbook: A Dramatic Approach to Literature*, rev. ed. (Glenview, IL: Scott Foresman, 1973), 151.

5. Ev Robertson, *The Dramatic Arts in Ministry* (Nashville: Convention Press, 1989), 48. Used by permission.

6. Charles M. Tanner, *Acting on Faith*, vol. 1 (Nashville: Abingdon, 1994), 9.

7. Steve Pederson, *Drama Ministry* (Grand Rapids: Zondervan, 1999), 146.

8. Laura Martinez, *Drama for the Dramatically Challenged: Church Plays Made Easy* (Valley Forge, PA: Judson Press, 2000), 7.

Stage Positions

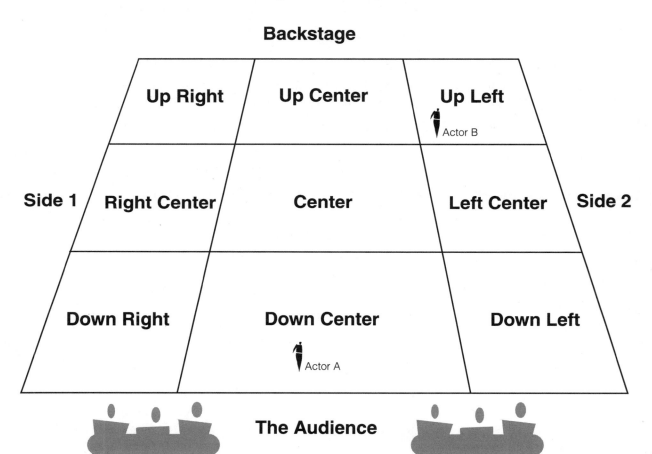

Left and right positions on the stage are designated from the actors' perspective, not the audience's. So if the script states that an actor enters stage right, he will enter from Side 1. Or if he needs to exit stage left, he will exit on Side 2.

Once an actor is onstage, he is standing in a designated position. If he is close to the audience or near the front of the stage, he is said to be in the "down" position or downstage. A position in the middle of the stage is called "center," and positions at the back of the stage are called "up." Actor A is close to the audience and is standing "down center," while Actor B is at the back of the stage and is standing "up left."

The Christmas Story
(Sketch)
Scripture references: Luke 2:1—39; Matthew 27—28

Theme: Christmas

Summary: Stage Manager becomes upset and frustrated with the Narrator who decides to give the church's traditional Christmas program a new twist by telling the story of the Crucifixion. The play concludes with the Narrator leading church members in a lively rap song showing that Christmas really is the Easter story because Jesus brought salvation to the world.

Characters:

Narrator: male

Stage Manager: female

Volunteer 1: female

Volunteer 2: male

Member 1: male or female

Member 2: male or female

Member 3: male or female

Child: boy or girl age 7 or younger

Costume Suggestions: Stage manager: all black. All others can wear Sunday attire.

Set Design/Props: Christmas season—simple or elaborate. A podium is downstage left, and two music stands or lecterns for holding scripts are at center stage. Other scenery may include Christmas decorations or a nativity scene.

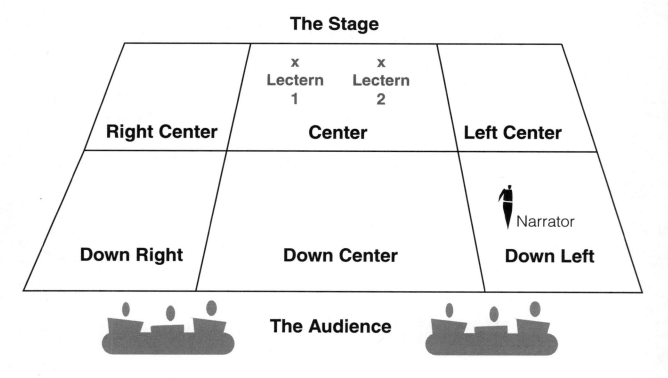

Rehearsal Notes:

The Christmas Story

Setting:

The following characters are seated at various places in the congregation:

Volunteer 1, Volunteer 2, Member 1, Member 2, and Member 3. The Child is sitting in the congregation near the front.

Stage Manager

(Enters stage right full of excitement) Welcome to our annual Christmas program! Our wonderful cast has worked hard to present to you this fantastic production. So sit back, relax, and enjoy this moving drama entitled "The Christmas Story." *(exits stage left)*

Narrator

(Enters stage left, goes to the podium down left, and begins reading) They came to a place called Golgotha, which means "the Place of the Skull." There they offered Jesus wine mixed with gall to drink, but after tasting it, he refused to drink it. When they had crucified him, they divided up his clothes by casting lots.

Stage Manager

(Runs onstage with a script in hand) Hey, wait a minute! *(apologetic to audience)* Oh, excuse me, but our narrator has the wrong script. *(to*

Narrator) Sorry about the mix-up. Here, read from this one. *(takes the script out of Narrator's hand and gives him a new one)*

(To audience) Excuse us. *(exits)*

Narrator

(Reading) And sitting down, they kept watch over him there. Above his head they placed the written charge against him, "This Is Jesus, The King of the Jews."

Member 1

(Stands) Hey, that's not the Christmas story. What about Mary and Joseph?

Stage Manager

(Runs onstage) What's going on?

Member 2

(Stands) And the three wise men from the East! *(sits)*

Member 3

(Stands) And the babe wrapped in swaddling clothing! *(sits)*

Member 1

And those shepherds who were watching their sheep by night. *(sits)*

Member 2

Don't forget "Hark! the Herald Angels Sing." We always sing "Hark! the Herald Angels Sing" at our annual Christmas program. *(sits)*

Stage Manager

(To the audience) People, people. Calm down. *(to Narrator, in frustration)* What do you think you're doing?

Narrator

Okay, okay, you want to hear about the angels, shepherds, Mary, and Joseph. So what happens after that?

Child

(Stands) Then we go home and wait for Santa Claus. Don't you know anything about Christmas? *(sits)*

Stage Manager

(Agitated) This is not what we rehearsed! They want to hear the Christmas story—just as we rehearsed.

Narrator

(To Stage Manager) All right, I agree. *(moving away from podium; to audience)* Since it's the Christmas season, it does make sense to tell the Christmas story. But I need some help.

Stage Manager

(Agitation increases) Help? I have the whole cast waiting backstage for their cue. Are you experiencing a strange case of stage fright or something? *(calming down)* Just get a grip. *(takes Narrator by the arm and leads him back to podium)* Now just take a deep breath and relax. Read the lines as we rehearsed them, and you'll be okay.

Narrator

(Moves away from the podium and talks to congregation) Since you know it so well, will someone from the congregation volunteer to tell the Christmas story?

Stage Manager

(Exasperated) You give a person a little chance to act, and he takes over. This Christmas program is a disaster. *(throws hands up in resignation and walks offstage)*

Volunteer 1

(Stands) I'll tell the story.

Volunteer 2

(Stands) And so will I.

Narrator

Good. Two volunteers. Come on up.

(Volunteer 1 and Volunteer 2 move toward the stage. Volunteer 1 talks to herself—but loud enough for others to hear—as she comes forward)

Volunteer 1

(Grumbling) I know the story like the back of my hand. Gracious! What kind of play is this where the narrator doesn't know the Christmas story?

Narrator

(Hands mike to Volunteer 1) It's all yours. Let's hear it.

Volunteer 1

(Snatches microphone and looks at Narrator in disgust and speaks self-assuredly) And Mary brought forth her firstborn Son, and wrapped him in swaddling clothes, and laid him in a manger, because there was no room for them in the inn. *(hands microphone to Volunteer 2)*

Volunteer 2

(Confidently) And there were in the same country shepherds abiding in the field, keeping watch over their flocks by night. And lo, the angel of the Lord came upon them.

Volunteers 1 and 2

And the glory of the Lord shone round about them; and they were sore afraid.

(Members 1, 2, 3 stand and applaud. Volunteers 1 and 2 take a bow)

Member 1

(Sitting) That's the story—

Member 2

Good! You're on right track now—*(sits)*

Member 3

Don't stop! We want to hear the rest of the story. *(sits)*

(Volunteer 2 hands microphone back to Narrator)

Volunteer 1

(To Narrator) Surely you can take the story from here.

Narrator

Great start! But I still need your help. *(hands script to Volunteer 1 and 2)* Here, take these scripts. And I will show you where I—

Volunteer 2

Script? I just volunteered to get you started. I'm not here to act in a play!

Volunteer 1

Oh, let's go on and be in the play. Just think, the sooner we do this, the sooner the program will be over and we can go home. I have to finish my Christmas shopping.

Volunteer 2

I suppose you have a good point there. I don't want to be here all day, and I certainly don't want to miss the football game. *(he reluctantly takes the script)*

Narrator

(Narrator goes to center stage and motions to Volunteer 1) Now you stand here. *(Volunteer 1 stands in front of one of the lecterns)*

Volunteer 1

Oh, this might be fun. *(looks stage right, searching for the Stage Manager and talks to herself)* I need the makeup artist to come out and touch me up. I want to look good.

Narrator

And sir, *(points to Volunteer 2)* you stand beside her.

(Volunteer 2 stands beside the second lectern)

Volunteer 1

Where's the stage manager? *(snaps fingers)* Stage manager! Makeup! Makeup, please!

(Stage Manager enters stage left carrying a furniture hand duster)

Just touch up my makeup a little. We're going to start soon. I want to look good up here.

(Stage Manager, totally agitated, takes the duster and abruptly slaps Volunteer 1's cheeks on the left and on the right. Stage Manger storms offstage)

What an attitude! It's so hard to find good makeup artists now days.

Narrator

All right. You read this part, *(points to Volunteer 1)* and sir, you read this. You got it?

Volunteer 2

Gotcha.

Volunteer 1

I'm ready.

Member 1

(Stands) And start at the beginning of the Christmas story, will you? *(sits)*

(Note to Director: The remaining portion of this sketch should be presented in rap style. Having musicians accompany the rap will really make it come to life.)

Narrator

One, two, ah one, two, three—

You say start at the beginning of the Christmas story

And that's just what we'll do.

To show how God Almighty revealed his glory

To save sinners like me and you.

It began with Adam and Eve and a tree nearby

Called the Knowledge of Good and Evil.

Volunteer 1

And a snake who said, "You shall not surely die."

This caused a complete upheaval.

Narrator

You see, Adam and Eve ate fruit from that tree

Like the sneaky snake told them to—

Volunteer 2

Now we're all sinners because they broke God's decree,

And there was only one thing God could do.

Narrator

They were punished, kicked out of this beautiful garden,

Since they disobeyed the Creator.

Because of their sin, they needed eternal pardon

Through a holy and righteous vindicator.

Now the whole human race was in a bad situation.

We no longer had a God connection.

Volunteer 2

Who can restore us, bring reconciliation

And heal this sin infection?

Volunteer 1

Who can save us from the bondage of sin—

And turn our life around?

Volunteer 2

Who can give us joy, sweet peace within—

And make grace and mercy abound?

Narrator

Jesus is the one. The Savior and King,

Who can make us whole again.

This good news makes angels sing,

And frees us from our sin.

Volunteers 1 and 2

"Hark! The herald angels sing,

Glory to the newborn King,

Peace on earth, and mercy mild."

All

"God and sinners reconciled!"

Narrator

You see, Christmas is the Easter story,

For Jesus mildly laid aside his glory—

To bring salvation down to earth,

Born to give us a new birth.

I say, "Hark! The herald angels sing."

Volunteer 1

"Glory to the newborn King."

Volunteer 2

"Peace on earth, and mercy mild."

All

"God and sinners reconciled!"

Volunteer 1

Reconciled?

Volunteer 2

Reconciled!

Volunteer 1

I must confess at first I was just playing,

But now I see what you're saying.

Jesus came to earth because of my sin,

What must I do to let him in?

Volunteer 2

"Hark! The herald angels sing,

Glory to the newborn King."

Second Adam from above,

Reinstate us in your love.

Narrator

You see, Christmas is the Easter story,

For Jesus mildly laid aside his glory—

To bring salvation down to earth,

Born to give us a new birth.

I say, "Hark! The herald angels sing."

Volunteer 1

"Glory to the newborn King."

Volunteer 2

"Peace on earth, and mercy mild."

All

"God and sinners reconciled!"

Member 3

(Stands) "God and sinners reconciled!"

Narrator

You got it!

Member 2

(Stands) "God and sinners reconciled!"

Narrator

That's it!

Member 1

(Stands) "God and sinners reconciled!"

Narrator

Say that!

All (including Members 1, 2, 3)

"God and sinners reconciled!"

(This could segue into the choir singing "Hark! the Herald Angels Sing" and the whole congregation joining in)

Lights Out!

A Mother's Love
(Recitation)

Scripture Reference: Proverbs 31:28

Theme: Mother's Day

Summary: This children's tribute tells us that a Mother's love is deeper and more beautiful than we are able to express.

Characters:

Older Child 1

Older Child 2

Older Child 3

Older Child 4

Younger Child 1

Younger Child 2

Younger Child 3

(Note: Include a balanced mix of girls and boys: older children—ages 8–12; younger children—age 7 or younger.)

Costume Suggestions: None required

Set Design: No particular place defined. The stage position is center.

(Note: The children will not need black folders with the script since all lines should be memorized.)

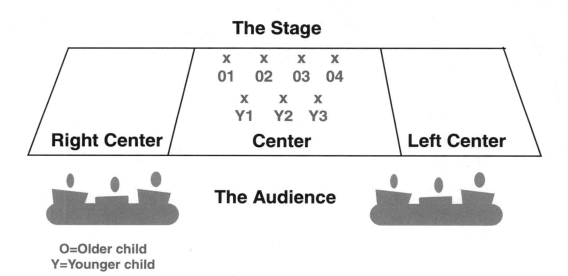

O=Older child
Y=Younger child

Rehearsal Notes:

A Mother's Love

Setting:

The children stand in a semicircle with the older children in the back.

Older Child 1

What poet can write enough verses to express the depth

Young Children

of a mother's love?

Older Child 2

What artist can draw all the beauty

Young Children

of a mother's love?

Older Child 3

And what orchestra has more harmony than that

Young Children

of a mother's love?

Older Child 4

Mothers are God's special gift to the world.

Older Child 1

Their love is an example of God's love for us.

Older Child 2

It is unconditional.

Young Child 1

Gentle.

Young Child 2

Kind.

Young Child 3

And patient.

Older Child 3

Today, mothers, we pay tribute to you.

Older Children

Thank you

Young Child 1

for your steadfast love.

Older Children

Thank you

Young Child 2

for teaching us right from wrong.

Older Children

Thank you

Older Child 4

for all your sacrifices,

Older Child 1

which are too many for us to count.

Older Child 2

We also remember mothers who are no longer with us.

Older Child 3

We remember you with our white carnations.

Young Children

We remember

Older Child 4

your words of wisdom.

Young Children

We remember

Older Child 1

all you taught us about God.

Older Child 2

As we close this tribute

Older Child 3

we want you to know that it expresses only a fraction of a mother's love.

Older Child 4

For no tribute can contain enough gratitude to acknowledge

Older Child 1

all the depth, all the beauty, and all the harmony

All

of a mother's love.

Older Children

May God bless you.

Young Children

We love you, mothers!

Lights Out!

The Husband Center
(Feature play)

Bible References: Proverbs 18:22; Philippians 4:11.

Themes: Single women, waiting on God, relationships

Summary: The year is 2050, and technology has advanced by leaps and bounds. The Husband Center is one by-product of this technology. Is it the solution for single women who want to get married? Or is it just another human invention that goes against biblical principles?

Characters:

Katrina Thomas: desperate for a husband

Renee Clemmons: sincere Christian unsure of The Husband Center

Diane: friend of Renee

Mrs. Sharon Jones: receptionist

Miss Pointer: Husband Center client

Mr. Arnold Miles: manufactured man

Dr. Ray: director of the Husband Center

Clinton: manufactured man

Costume Suggestions: All characters may wear contemporary clothing. Optional: futuristic/science fiction–like attire

Set Design: Medical center. A setting that resembles a doctor's office atmosphere. Large posters of men in various professions may be displayed (doctor, lawyer, judge, policeman, etc.).

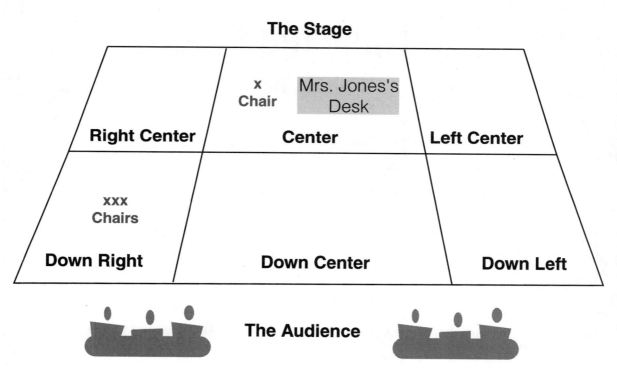

The Stage

x
Chair

Mrs. Jones's Desk

Right Center   **Center**   **Left Center**

xxx
Chairs

Down Right   **Down Center**   **Down Left**

The Audience

Rehearsal Notes:

The Husband Center

Setting:

Center stage is a receptionist desk where Mrs. Jones is sitting. She is busy with paperwork. Beside her desk is a chair. Down right are three more chairs.

(Renee and Diane enter. Diane takes a seat, and Renee walks to Mrs. Jones's desk)

Mrs. Jones

(To Renee) Welcome to The Husband Center. How may I help you today? Would you like to complete an application?

Renee

(Uncertain) Yes. Ah—well, . . . actually I would like to know more about the process before I complete an application. *(phone rings)*

Mrs. Jones

Of course you would. I'm Mrs. Jones, and you are . . .

Renee

Renee, Renee Clemmons. *(phone rings)*

Mrs. Jones

Miss Clemmons, here's an application. Complete the first page, and I'll explain everything in just a minute.

(Renee takes the application and sits down beside Diane)

Mrs. Jones

(Answers phone cheerfully) Hello. The Husband Center—where she who finds a husband finds a good thing. Yes, we do offer affordable men. . . . You're interested in a Methodist man with a little bit of Pentecostal mixed in? I got you. *(confident)* We can do that, just come on in to the center. . . . Thanks for calling.

(Mrs. Jones stands and walks to Renee and Diane) All right, ladies, let me explain how we do things. *(looks at Diane)* Miss, do you need an application?

Diane

No thanks. I'm happily married. *(points to Renee)* I'm here with my friend for moral support.

Mrs. Jones

Here at The Husband Center our qualified staff of geneticists and biochemists create the man of your dreams using a combination of cloning and artificial intelligence.

Renee

And these are real men, right?

Mrs. Jones

Honey, they're as real as they come. You're not living back in the dark ages of the 1980s. This *is* 2050, and technology now is phenomenal. Take a look at the application, page 2. As you can see, it has a list of specifications and characteristics that you may want in a husband. If you want a husband who is wealthy, just check the box. If you want a man who has a wonderful sense of humor, just check the box. If you want a man who loves to travel, what do you do?

Diane

Just check the box.

Mrs. Jones

You got it, sister. We can create a man who will love, respect, and honor you for the rest of your life.

Diane

Hel-lo. That's your kind of man, Renee.

Mrs. Jones

You got that right. I'm talking about your man. And if there's a characteristic you want that's not listed, just add it.

Renee

(Thoughtful) So . . . you have the capability of creating a spiritual man? I mean a man who is a genuine Christian?

Mrs. Jones

Oh my goodness, yes. In fact, we are one of only three centers in the world that create Christian men. Honey, this place is a gold mine. You can even specify the denomination—*(rolls the denominations off her tongue quickly)* Methodist, Baptist, Presbyterian, Catholic, Pentecostal, whatever. *(explains enthusiastically)* So after you finish your application, bring it back to me with a deposit. And that's it. You can leave. I will give this paperwork to our very competent scientists in the lab, and they will create the man of your dreams. We will call you when your man is ready. Then you will pay the balance and come pick up your own tailor-made man.

Diane

(Gives Renee a friendly tap on the arm) Girl, you hear that? This is what you've been looking for.

Renee

How long will it take?

Mrs. Jones

Good question. That varies depending on the specifications you request. It can take anywhere from two weeks to a year.

(Miss Pointer and Arnold Miles, a well-dressed man and woman, enter stage left. Both are wearing business attire. Miss Pointer has several sheets of paper in her hand. Mrs. Jones notices the couple; Renee and Diane have their eyes on Arnold)

Mrs. Jones

Oh, Miss Pointer, you look like you're ready to leave *(eyes Arnold up and down)* with your well-crafted package here.

Arnold

(Speaks to Renee and Diane) Praise the Lord, sisters. God is so good, isn't he?

Renee

(Smiles sincerely) Yes, he is.

Diane

(Sexy voice) All the time.

Mrs. Jones

See, ladies, *(points to Arnold)* here's an example of what the center can do for you. *(speaks to Miss Pointer)* I'll sign off on your paperwork, and then you and Mr. Miles are free to go.

Diane

Oh, Lord, he's good-looking! *(elbows Renee)* Girl, look at him.

Renee

Yes, he is handsome.

(Dr. Ray enters)

Mrs. Jones

(Signs the papers and hands a copy to Miss Pointer) Okay, here's your copy.

Dr. Ray

We appreciate your coming to the center. I know you're going to be totally satisfied with Mr. Miles here.

Miss Pointer

(Polished and professional tone) This addition to my life is going to enhance my career greatly. Thank you, Dr. Ray, for your superb service. *(they shake hands)*

(Miss Pointer and Arnold leave)

Arnold

(Speaks to Miss Pointer) Honey, I'm going to love you like Christ loved the church. I'm going to protect you with my life.

(Renee and Diane respond simultaneously)

Renee

Whoaa. Oh my goodness.

Diane

(High-pitched, joyful voice) Glorrrrrry! Now that man is saying something.

Miss Pointer

That's so sweet, Arnold.

(Arnold and Miss Pointer exit)

Renee

So how much did he cost?

Mrs. Jones

(Looks at Renee) Let's just say Miss Pointer paid some hefty bucks for Arnold. He was one of our one-year projects. I assure you, Miss Clemmons, we can provide a man just like that for you. Now, if you will complete your application, I will help you as soon as you're ready. Just take your time. You are creating your future husband here, and you don't want a rush job.

Renee

Thank you.

(Mrs. Jones walks to her desk. Katrina enters wearing business attire. She is obviously in a hurry. She walks to Mrs. Jones's desk)

Katrina

(Impatient) I would like to place an order. I already know the kind of man I want, so I hope this won't take long.

Mrs. Jones

Well, you've come to the right place. *(hands her an application)* Here you go. Complete this, and let me know if you have any questions.

Katrina

(Flips through the eight-page application in disappointment) This is a book. How long will it take? I need to get this done on my lunch hour, and I only have forty-five minutes.

Mrs. Jones

(Struggling to be diplomatic) It's going to take longer than forty-five minutes, and you have one person ahead of you.

Renee

She can go ahead of me, Mrs. Jones. I'm not sure if this is something I want to do.

Diane

(Upset) Not sure! What do you mean, Renee? *(Renee and Diane talk quietly)*

Katrina

You see, I really don't need an application. I have this list.

(Katrina opens a folder and unrolls a sheet of paper that reaches to the floor. She hands it to Mrs. Jones. Mrs. Jones studies the list as Katrina rambles on)

I'm going to my high school reunion in three weeks, and I must be married before then. I mean, I just turned thirty this year, and there's no way I'm going to that reunion still single. Can you imagine me walking in there alone? The—

Mrs. Jones

What is your name, miss?

Katrina

Katrina Thomas.

Mrs. Jones

Miss Thomas, from the characteristics and qualities you have listed here, you certainly have created the perfect Christian husband, but we cannot make him in three weeks.

Katrina

You can't? Don't you do rush orders? I'm willing to pay extra if I need to. How much is he going to cost anyway?

Mrs. Jones

Our basic man starts at eight hundred dollars.

(Renee and Diane stop talking and begin listening to Katrina and Mrs. Jones's conversation)

Katrina

Oh, I can work with that. So do I pay you now or later?

Mrs. Jones

Miss Thomas, let me explain. When I say basic, I mean basic—just a warm body. Each individual characteristic that you add is a charge. For example, on your list you have that he must be wealthy. Well, a wealthy man, depending on how wealthy you want him to be, is going to automatically add five thousand dollars or more to the price.

Katrina

Okay, bottom line. *(looks at watch)* I have nine hundred dollars to work with, so I'll take a good, Christian, Spirit-filled man for that price.

Diane

That's right, sister. You order your man.

Mrs. Jones

(Shakes head) Again, Miss Thomas—

Katrina

Please stop calling me Miss Thomas. That's why I'm here—so I can get a husband and change my name to Mrs. Just call me Katrina.

Mrs. Jones

(Agitated but keeps her composure) Katrina, according to your list, you want a man who will live a holy life and love God and you with all his heart. The price for that quality starts at eight thousand dollars, and that's the minimum.

Katrina

Eight thousand dollars? I can't afford that!

Mrs. Jones

(Matter-of-factly) There's a high price for holiness, you know.

Katrina

I thought this was a Christian center. Doesn't that eight hundred dollars I'm paying at least include a Christian man?

Mrs. Jones

For eight hundred dollars you will get a man who might go with you to church on Easter. No guarantee. If you want a churchgoing man, one who will go to church with you every Sunday, that's an extra one hundred dollars.

Diane

Go on and pay that extra one hundred dollars, sister. You don't want to go to church alone every Sunday.

Katrina

(Looks at watch) Well, that's not important as long as he respects me.

Mrs. Jones

You will have to pay between three hundred dollars and ten thousand dollars for respect, depending on the level.

Katrina

I just don't have that kind of money. But you know what? *(speaks as if trying to convince herself)* I know myself. I am a very persuasive person. I can change him. I'll teach him how to respect me.

Mrs. Jones

There you go. That's right—you can change him. I tell people all the time that if they can't afford the man they want, then don't worry about it. Just change him.

Diane

No, you can't. You can't change a grown man.

Mrs. Jones

Miss, you are disturbing my client and me. So could you please keep your comments to yourself? *(speaks to Katrina convincingly)* A little sweet talk—you know how to do it—and girl, he'll change.

Katrina

Okay, I'll just order a basic man for eight hundred dollars.

Mrs. Jones

(Smiles) Oh, I'm so glad we can help you, Katrina. Oh, I meant Mrs. Katrina. I'll write up your order for a basic man. You said your budget was nine hundred dollars. Are there any other qualities you want to add?

Katrina

I assume he'll have a job, right?

Mrs. Jones

A man with a job is an additional cost, and depending on the type of job, it starts at three hundred fifty dollars and goes up from there.

Katrina

I only have an extra one hundred dollars. *(looks at watch)* Forget the job. I'll help him find a job.

Diane

Sister girl, you'd better get a man with a job.

Mrs. Jones

Yes, you can help him find work. That will save you some money.

Diane

Don't pay for a man who doesn't work. In fact, I wouldn't pay for anything that didn't work.

Mrs. Jones

Miss, if you continue your outburst, I will have to ask you to leave.

Renee

Diane, just be cool.

Diane

(Lowers voice, but loud enough for audience to hear) Well, it's the truth. I wouldn't pay for anything that didn't work. I wouldn't pay for a postal stamp that didn't work. I wouldn't pay for a paper clip that didn't work.

Katrina

There is one other characteristic that I want. I want a man who knows how to cook.

Mrs. Jones

Well, Katrina, you're in business. For one hundred dollars you can get a man who can cook dinner very well.

Katrina

Praise the Lord!

Mrs. Jones

That total then is nine hundred dollars. In fact, we may have a man in our lab already made that you can take with you today. You just complete this vital information, and I'll check with Dr. Ray in the lab.

Katrina

Great! Oh, I can't believe it. *(continues to write and speaks to herself)* I am actually going to get married Sunday. I have my wedding already planned. *(she digs in her purse and pulls out a compact and begins to primp)* I've got to look good for my honey. *(begins to sing the tune of "Here Comes the Bride")* Here comes the bride. *(hums the tune)* Hmm, hmmm, hmm, hmmm. Dum, dum, dum, dum.

Diane

(To Renee) Dumb is right! That she is—dumb.

(Mrs. Jones returns with Dr. Ray beside her. When Katrina sees Dr. Ray her face lights up)

Mrs. Jones

Katrina, this is Dr. Ray.

Katrina

(Gives him a hug) Oh my! My man is a doctor too. You're more than I could ever want in a husband.

Dr. Ray

Excuse me, miss. I am—

Mrs. Jones

Katrina, Dr. Ray is the director of The Husband Center. He's not the man you ordered. Clinton is the man you—*(looks around)* Where's Clinton? I thought he was right beside you, Dr. Ray.

Dr. Ray

(Looks behind him) He's on his way now. *(shakes Katrina's hand)* Miss Thomas, congratulations, and I know you will be completely satisfied. *(Clinton appears and is wearing jeans, a T-shirt, shades, and a cap with the bib turned backwards)*

Katrina

Thank you, Dr. Ray. *(looks at Clinton)* You have made me the happiest woman on earth.

Clinton

So where is my woman?

Mrs. Jones

Clinton, this is Katrina Thomas. She's taking you home with her today. *(Dr. Ray exits)*

Clinton

(Looks at Renee and Diane) There be some good-looking women around here. *(speaks to Renee)* Hey, sweetie, take me home with you.

Katrina

(Pulls Clinton away from Renee) Now, honey, you're going home with me. *(still pulling on him as they walk stage left)*

Mrs. Jones

Katrina, you just need to sign your papers, pay your fee, and then you can be off to romantic bliss.

(Katrina goes to Mrs. Jones's desk to complete the paperwork)

Katrina

(To Clinton) Now, I have to go back to work, but you can come with me to fill out a job application. There are several job openings where I work.

Clinton

(Laughs hysterically) Job? *(continues laughing)* I ain't working for nobody. *(sternly)* *You* got a job, so *you* can pay the bills.

Katrina

Oh, don't get upset, Clinton. I can take care of both of us right now. *(looks at her watch)* Oh my, I got to get back to work. *(takes out her keys)*

Clinton

Let me see those keys. I'm driving.

Katrina

Thank you, sweetie. *(ecstatic)* I got a man to chauffeur me around too! I'm in heaven! *(puts her arm around Clinton)* I look forward to your delicious meals. I understand you are an excellent cook.

Clinton

(*Boastfully*) You got that right. I'm a master chef. I can cook a killer meatloaf, a sho 'nuff slap-your-lips potato salad, steamed cabbage, sweet potato pie. . . . But I ain't cooking for you. The woman is suppose to cook, not the man.

Katrina

(*Looks at Mrs. Jones*) But I paid that extra one hundred dollars for—

Mrs. Jones

(*Speaks in a whisper as if embarrassed for Katrina*) You paid for a man who knows *how* to cook. But you have to pay an additional one hundred dollars for a man who has a *desire* to cook for you. (*she throws her hands in the air in resignation and gives a phony, empathic face*)

Katrina

What?

Mrs. Jones

But don't you worry about it, Katrina. Remember, you can change him. (*gives a phony grin*)

Clinton

(*Grabs Katrina by the arm*) Let's get out of here. Get . . . out . . . of . . . here . . . (*Clinton's voice changes to a robotic sound, and he continues to say, "get out of here," as the conversation continues*) Get . . . out . . . of . . . here . . .

Katrina

Oh no, he's defective!

Diane

Girl, I could have told you that.

Katrina

What's wrong?

Mrs. Jones

Oh, sometimes the men have little quirks like stuttering, but don't worry; it doesn't happen that often. All you have to do is just give him a firm slap in the chest *(she slaps him in the chest, and Clinton stops saying "get out of here")* and he's back to normal.

(Clinton shakes head as if startled)

Clinton

What are we doing here? I got to hit the road.

Katrina

Praise the Lord. He's back to normal. Let's go, honey. *(takes Clinton by the hand)*

Mrs. Jones

(Waves to Katrina and Clinton) Oh, you two are a cute couple. Have a beautiful wedding and a fantastic life.

Clinton

(Walking offstage) Wedding? What you talking 'bout? I ain't marrying you!

(By this time Clinton and Katrina are offstage. Mrs. Jones goes back to her desk)

Mrs. Jones

Oh, Katrina! Katrina! *(runs to try to catch her)* I guess she's gone. I forgot to tell her that Clinton doesn't know how to drive. Oh, well. Renee, take all the time you need to complete your application. I have to go get some files, and I'll be right back. *(exits stage left)*

Diane

Now that girl was desperate with a capital D.

(Renee shakes her head and is in deep thought. Diane looks at Renee)

What's wrong with you? *(suddenly realizes what's wrong)* Oh, don't say it. I know what you're going to say. I have heard the same ol' line—

(Renee looks at Diane in frustration, and Diane stares back at her with an upset face)

Renee and Diane

This is not God's will.

Diane

(Sarcastic) This is not God's will. Well, what is God's will? Renee, you need to get in touch with the times. You're not living in our parents' time, back in the 1990s. This is 2050! Take advantage of this wonderful technology. You think the Christian matchmaking services are worldly. I tried to set you up with some very nice guys, but they weren't good enough for you.

Renee

Diane, those guys were nice, but they weren't Christians. I want to marry someone who is at least going in the same direction I'm going.

Diane

You know what your problem is? You are just too picky. You are looking for the perfect man.

Renee

No, I'm not. I just want God's best for me.

Diane

How do you know that this is not God's best?

Renee

It can't be. The motto of this center misquotes Scripture: "She who finds a husband"? The Bible says, "He who finds a wife finds a good thing." My husband is supposed to find me.

Diane

Well, he must be lost, because it's taking him a long time to find you. *(upset)* So you're not going to do this?

Renee

I just need to think about this.

Diane

(Annoyed but tries to remain calm) Well, this is my vacation day. And I took this time off to support you because I know you want to get married. *(annoyance turns to concern)* Renee, you will be forty years old next year, and you have never been married. I'm not saying you can't find a good Christian man out there in the world, but ... what if ... what if you never get married?

Renee

I'll keep on living for God, Diane. I can't put my life on hold. God has plans and purposes for me to fulfill.

Diane

Girl, you're a better woman than I am. If God had told me I'd never marry, I would be one angry sister. I tell you what, Renee. I'm going to go. Maybe you need to think about this by yourself. I really want you to do it only because you deserve a good Christian man, but you'll have to make that decision. *(stands)* Call me later, okay?

Renee

Okay, girl. See you later.

(Diane leaves; Renee sits in her seat in deep thought)

Dr. Ray

(Enters, goes to Mrs. Jones's desk, and picks up a file; as he looks through the file, he notices Renee sitting in contemplation) Mrs. Jones

will be back to help you shortly. How are you coming along with your application, young lady? It's in-depth paperwork, I know, but I'm sure you will be pleased with the finished product.

(Renee gives Dr. Ray a blank stare)

Dr. Ray

Is something wrong? Are there any questions I can answer?

Renee

Dr. Ray, are you married?

Dr. Ray

(Surprised) Ah . . . yes. Yes, I am.

Renee

Is she a robot?

Dr. Ray

Excuse me?

Renee

She's not artificial is she, like the men you are creating in this lab?

Dr. Ray

No. She's not.

Renee

You know, I don't want an artificial man, a man-made invention either. Just like God blessed you with a real woman, I want God to bring a real Christian man into my life. I can't go through with this. *(she stands)*

Dr. Ray

Well, I certainly will not try to force you to stay. But you did take the time to at least come in. Out of curiosity, why did you come in today?

Renee

I just felt like I had waited long enough for a husband. And two months ago, I obtained custody of my sister's two children. She's in prison. Taking care of the kids—and the way it looks, I'll have them for a long time—I just felt overwhelmed. I felt like I needed a man to help me. And I didn't want *any* man, but a good Christian husband.

Dr. Ray

That's the reason this center is here. I feel like I have fulfilled my job when I see Christian women like yourself being matched with good Christian men.

Renee

(Walks toward the door) Well, I suppose your heart is in the right place, Dr. Ray, but this is not for me.

(Phone rings)

Dr. Ray

If you change your mind, come back to see us. You can leave the application on the desk.

(While Dr. Ray is on the phone, Renee gathers her purse and papers)

(Answers phone) Hello, The Husband Center. The place where she who finds a husband finds a good thing. May I help you? . . . Our prices vary. *(Renee places application on the desk)* . . . We could have the man completed in a few weeks, or it could take as long as a year. . . . Oh, I see. So how long are you willing to wait for a husband? How long are you . . . willing . . . to . . . wait . . . for . . . a . . . husband? *(Renee turns around and stares at Dr. Ray in shock. His voice slows to a robotic sound)*

How long . . . are . . . you . . . willing . . . to . . . wait . . . for . . . a . . . husband. . . . willing . . . to . . . wait . . . for . . . a husband . . . wait for a husband . . . wait.

Lights Out!

What People Think
(Readers theater)

Scripture Reference: Proverbs 29:25

Theme: Fear of what others think

Summary: This readers theater reveals how we often make decisions based on our fear of people and what they think, rather than on what God wants us to do. This drama is not meant to stand alone but will work best when presented as a sermon starter for a worship service or as an introduction to a small group discussion. A sermon starter is simply a short dramatic presentation that illuminates and illustrates the message. The Devotional Moment at the end helps bring resolve to the reading and could be an avenue for further discussion for small groups.

Characters:

Speaker 1: male

Speaker 2: male or female

Speaker 3: female

Set Design: No specific place defined. Three stools are arranged in a semicircle at center stage.

Props: Black folders with scripts for each speaker and music stands (if the drama is not memorized)

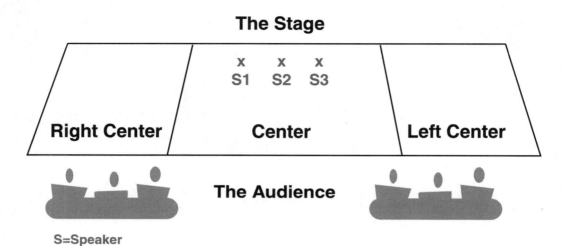

S=Speaker

Rehearsal Notes:

What People Think

Setting:

Speakers 1, 2, and 3 are sitting on stools.

All

We are the people.

And we think. *(speakers pose, as if thinking)*

Speaker 1

We think a lot.

Speaker 2

We think about everything *(points to audience)* you do.

Speaker 3

And we have something to say about it too.

Speaker 1

(Pondering) I've been thinking about starting my own business.

Speaker 3

John is thinking about starting a new business. He must be crazy.

Speaker 2

I know that's right. He would be a fool to leave his job with such a good salary—

Speakers 1 and 2

And benefits.

Speaker 2

And he has a family to support too. What a big—

Speaker 1

Risk . . . yeah, that's crazy. I mean, what will people think, if I left my job?

All

We are the people,

And we think.

Speaker 2

We think about you.

Speaker 1

Hey, why not? We have nothing else to do.

Speaker 2

Sunday is the big day for me. I have to lead a solo in the choir. I'm so nervous.

Speaker 1

And indeed you should be.

Speaker 3

What if you sing off-key?

Speaker 1

That would look pretty bad.

Speakers 1 and 3

And besides . . .

Speaker 2

I've never led a song before. And I can't sing as well as—

All

We are the people,

And we think.

Speaker 2

We just think all the time.

Speaker 1

Yes indeed, twenty-four–seven.

Speaker 3

And we are thinking about . . .

All

(Point at audience) You!

Speaker 1

(Nonchalant) We have nothing else to do.

Speaker 3

I'm engaged. God has blessed me with a—

Speaker 1

Now, I can't believe you're marrying him.

Speaker 2

And I can't believe he's marrying her.

Speaker 1

Why, he is—

Speaker 2

And she is—

Speaker 1

And he doesn't have—

Speaker 2

And she is just too—

Speaker 3

Yeah, you're right.

All

We are the people.

And we—

Speaker 1

They know what we do by now.

Speaker 3

Now that you know what we do,

Perhaps we can think for you.

Speaker 2

What are your plans?

Speaker 1

What decisions do you have to make?

Speaker 3

Do you need an opinion?

Speaker 2

Let us help you plan your next event.

All

We're on call twenty-four–seven.

Speaker 1

And our number is listed everywhere.

Speaker 3

And if you don't call us—

Speaker 2

We *will* call you.

All

And tell you what we think!

Lights Out!

Devotional Moment

Fear of man will prove to be a snare, but whoever trusts in the LORD is kept safe.   Proverbs 29:25

A fear of people, specifically what people think, is a primary hindrance for many Christians. "What will people think?" we often ask ourselves when faced with a decision. But living in fear of what people think creates a trap that can immobilize us, hindering us from fulfilling God's purpose and thus causing us to settle for less.

A better question to ask is, "What does God think?" And if God approves—no matter how odd or irrational it may look to others—then we are "safe," as Proverbs 29:25 states. We are safe because we have not only God's support in completing the task, whether great or small, but also his protection. What security God brings. *Now think about it.*

Other Scriptures

Psalm 56:11
Romans 8:37
Philippians 4:13
Hebrews 13:6

The Curator
(Sketch)

Scripture References: Psalm 103:12; Isaiah 43:25; 2 Corinthians 5:17; Ephesians 1:7

Themes: Forgiveness, redemption, and handling failures

Summary: This sketch shows how we often hold on to our failures, guilt, and shame, creating a mental museum of our pain. God, on the other hand, stands ready to forgive us and offers us peace for our mind, enabling us to live a new life with Jesus Christ. This sketch is not meant to stand alone but will work well when presented as a sermon starter for a worship service or as an introduction to a small group discussion. A sermon starter is simply a short dramatic presentation that illuminates and illustrates the message. The Devotional Moment at the end of this sketch helps bring resolve to the sketch and could be an avenue for further discussion for small groups.

Characters:

Marilyn Lester: museum curator

Elaine Sanders: museum guest

Set Design: A museum—simple or elaborate. One simple way to design the set is to use a small folding table for each collection. Display a poster or sign in front of each table that includes the name of the collection. Place a few items representative of the collection on the table. For example, the Family Generation Collection might have stacks of prescription medicine bottles and other medicine.

   Props: A ring, baking utensils (baking pans, a mixer, and so forth), recipe books, an obituary

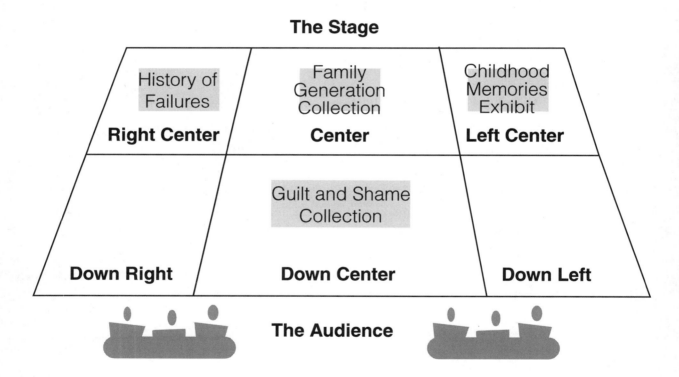

Rehearsal Notes:

The Curator

Setting:

Elaine is at center stage examining the Family Generation Collection.

Marilyn

(Enters stage right) Sorry to keep you waiting, Mrs. Sanders. *(shakes Elaine's hand)* I'm Marilyn Lester, museum curator.

Elaine

Oh, please just call me Elaine.

Marilyn

Thank you again for choosing my museum as a gift recipient. You see, this place has been a self-supporting institution all these years.

Elaine

Oh, I'm delighted. *(looking around)* So this is it! The Marilyn Lester Museum. When do we begin the tour?

Marilyn

We can start right here with the History of Failures. *(goes right center to Failures collection)*

Elaine

Hmmm. What a huge failure collection. What do we have here? *(examines collection)* I see you enrolled in college but dropped out.

Marilyn

My mother always said I never completed anything in life. And she was right. I think I've failed at everything.

Elaine

Oh, look at these wonderful artifacts—recipes, baking pans, a mixer. It looks like you had a bakery at some point.

Marilyn

Three years ago I had my own baking business.

Elaine

(Picks up a sheet of paper and reads) Marilyn's Sweet Shop.

Marilyn

Yes, and that didn't work out either.

(Elaine looks at another collection)

Elaine

(Holds up an item) And this ring is absolutely beautiful. It must have cost a fortune.

Marilyn

That's my wedding ring. Too bad the marriage wasn't as beautiful as the ring.

Elaine

How long were you married?

Marilyn

Five years. Well, actually four. We lived together for a year. *(reminiscing)* Thomas Lester. *(pauses and sighs)* Now that man was one of my biggest failures.

Elaine

What happened?

Marilyn

I'll just say the love went out. It went out to all the women that Thomas could get his hands on. *(angry)* That sorry, *(angrier)* good for nothing— I don't even want to waste my breath talking about him. Okay ... we have been in the failures collection long enough.

Elaine

(Looking around) Investment failures, bad relationships—

Marilyn

(Moves Elaine along) Okay, Elaine, lets move on out of failures. *(moves stage center)* And this is the Family Generation Collection.

Elaine

Hmm. *(concerned)* You've had a long line of relatives suffer with depression, haven't you?

Marilyn

Do I need to tell you how many pills I take every day just to make it?

Elaine

(Moves left center) Oh, look at this. Here's your Childhood Memories Exhibit. *(curious)* But it says the collection is closed.

Marilyn

I've had my Childhood Exhibit closed for sometime now.

Elaine

So when will you display it again?

Marilyn

(Pauses, then speaks in a somber tone) Never. Probably ... never. My childhood was terrible. I can't even talk about it. Well, let's move on to the Guilt and Shame Collection. *(moves down center)*

Elaine

(Looks at sign and reads) "Guilt and Shame Collection." Oh, Marilyn, I think this must be your largest exhibit. *(studies obituary)* Hmm, your father's obituary. You look just like him.

Marilyn

That's what everyone says. *(regretful)* I never should have said those awful words to him.

Elaine

What awful words, Marilyn? Did the two of you get along?

Marilyn

No. We were never close. He was . . . well, I won't get into that. Anyway, we had a bad argument, the real knock-down-drag-out type, and I said to him. . . , *(hesitant)* "I wish you were dead." *(takes deep breath)* Well, two weeks later, he died. He was in a terrible car accident.

Elaine

Oh, I'm sorry to hear that.

Marilyn

Yes . . . I'm sorry about that too. I've replayed that argument in my mind every day for the past twelve years. *(trying to perk up)* Okay, enough of the Shame Collection. Let's move on, because there's just too much in here for me to think about. I've probably already bored you with the history of my life anyway.

Elaine

Not at all. Please continue.

Marilyn

Let's see. *(looks around)* What should I show you next? I have more exhibits, but my curiosity is killing me, Elaine. Most organizations normally tell the amount of their donation or exactly what gift they're offering, but you haven't. So . . . what *is* the gift?

Elaine

I'm not representing any particular organization. I'm just here on my own. The gift is the precious blood, the blood of Jesus Christ.

Marilyn

(Shocked) Blood! *(calming down)* That's very kind of you, but the Red Cross is just two blocks down the street. They are always looking for people to donate blood.

Elaine

Not my blood, the blood of Jesus, Marilyn. Jesus died on the cross to restore our relationship with God.

Marilyn

I don't understand.

Elaine

When Adam and Eve sinned, they broke the fellowship they had with God. Now we are all sinners. It is only through Jesus that we can be connected back to God again. I see your struggle in preserving your history of failures, guilt, and shame. It's too much for you to do alone.

Marilyn

Tell me about it. I need to hire someone to work part-time around here. There's always a new failure to record.

Elaine

But that's just it. We don't have to continue keeping track of all our mistakes. Jesus shed his blood on the cross to give us a whole new life. And this new life is the gift Jesus offers—eternal life. He will forgive us of everything if we just ask. All Jesus wants you to do is give all this pain and hopelessness stored here to him.

Marilyn

He wants my museum? Oh, I can't give this up. This is my life. *(reflective)* It's a burden at times, but it's all I know. *(justifying)* And it's not too bad—being reminded of my failures keeps me from making the same mistakes.

Elaine

But God will not remind you of your failures ever again. Jesus can set you free of all this guilt and shame. I'm not saying you will never experience problems. But Jesus will give you strength to endure and to overcome any difficult situation.

Marilyn

You sound so certain. How do you know Jesus can do all of this? You want me to rely on a God who is out there . . . in heaven . . . *(unsure)* or somewhere. If I didn't know any better, I would think you knew God personally. And surely that's not possible, is it?

Lights Out!

Devotional Moment

In him we have redemption through his blood, the forgiveness of sins, in accordance with the riches of God's grace.   Ephesians 1:7

As far as the east is from the west, so far has he removed our transgressions from us   Psalm 103:12

Therefore, if anyone is in Christ, he is a new creation; the old has gone, the new has come!   2 Corinthians 5:17

I, even I, am he who blots out your transgressions, for my own sake, and remembers your sins no more.   Isaiah 43:25

Questions for Reflection

1. Why is it often difficult to forgive ourselves of our failures and sins?
2. When we ask God for forgiveness, what does he do with our sins?
3. Does having a personal relationship with Jesus make it easier for a person to forgive himself/herself as well as forgive others? Why, or why not?
4. How would you explain 1 Corinthians 5:17 to a person who isn't a Christian?
5. Are there any failures for which you have created a "mental museum"? If so, offer a prayer to God, asking him to help you release your heart and mind of these defeats.

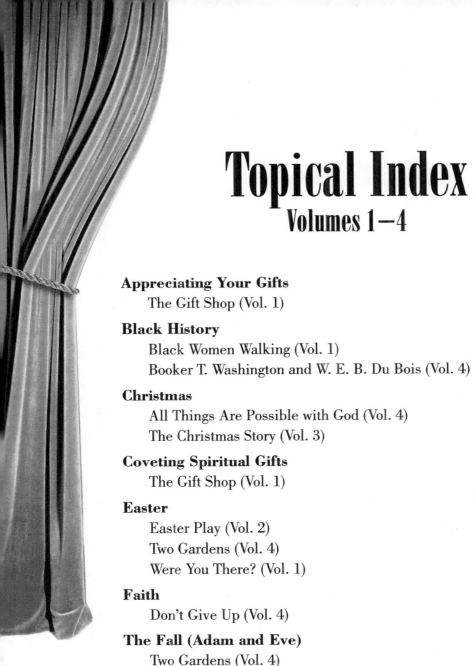

Topical Index
Volumes 1–4

Appreciating Your Gifts
The Gift Shop (Vol. 1)

Black History
Black Women Walking (Vol. 1)
Booker T. Washington and W. E. B. Du Bois (Vol. 4)

Christmas
All Things Are Possible with God (Vol. 4)
The Christmas Story (Vol. 3)

Coveting Spiritual Gifts
The Gift Shop (Vol. 1)

Easter
Easter Play (Vol. 2)
Two Gardens (Vol. 4)
Were You There? (Vol. 1)

Faith
Don't Give Up (Vol. 4)

The Fall (Adam and Eve)
Two Gardens (Vol. 4)

Forgiveness
> The Curator (Vol. 3)
> Watch What You Hold On To (Vol. 2)

God's Provision
> God's Provision (Vol. 1)

Handling Failures
> The Curator (Vol. 3)

Hope
> Don't Give Up (Vol. 4)

Hypocrisy
> Easter Play (Vol. 2)
> How Is Your Quiet Time? (Vol. 1)
> The Spiritual Bank (Vol. 2)

Judging Others
> How Is Your Quiet Time? (Vol. 1)

Love
> Is It Love or Noise? (Vol. 2)

Male/Female Relationships
> The Husband Center (Vol. 3)

Mother's Day
> A Mother's Love (Vol. 3)

People Pleasers
> What People Think (Vol. 3)

Persistence
> Don't Give Up (Vol. 4)

Power of Words
>   Tongue Twisters (Vol. 2)

Salvation/Redemption
>   The Curator (Vol. 3)
>   Two Gardens (Vol. 4)

Single Women
>   The Husband Center (Vol. 3)

Sunday School
>   Come to Sunday School (Vol. 4)

Vain Worship and Works
>   The Spiritual Bank (Vol. 2)

Women
>   Black Women Walking (Vol. 1)

We want to hear from you. Please send your comments about this book to us in care of zreview@zondervan.com. Thank you.

GRAND RAPIDS, MICHIGAN 49530 USA

W W W . Z O N D E R V A N . C O M